MAGGIE LANE'S BOOK OF BEADS

Books by Maggie Lane

Needlepoint by Design
More Needlepoint by Design
Chinese Rugs Designed for Needlepoint
Rugs and Wall Hangings
Maggie Lane's Pillows
Maggie Lane's Oriental Patchwork
Maggie Lane's Book of Beads

MAGGIE LANE'S BOOK OF BEADS

Charles Scribner's Sons   New York

*This book is dedicated to the memory of
my dear friend Mina Shaughnessy*

Copyright © 1979 Maggie Lane

Library of Congress Cataloging in Publication Data

Lane, Maggie.
Maggie Lane's Book of beads.

Bibliography: p. 63
1. Beadwork. 2. Necklaces. 3. Knots and splices.
I. Title. II. Title: Book of beads.
TT860.L36   745.59'42   79-12126
ISBN 0-684-16234-2

1 3 5 7 9 11 13 15 17 19 G/P 20 18 16 14 12 10 8 6 4 2

Printed in the United States of America

Contents

Preface   7

Introduction   9

Materials   13

Tinting or Dyeing the Cord   15

Knots   17

    Types of Knots   17
    One-Cord Knotting   17
    Two-Cord Knotting   20
    Three-Cord Knotting   30

The Necklaces   39

    "Necklace" Necklace   41
    Anastasia   42
    Spring   42
    Gypsy   43
    Pendant Necklace in Silver Bamboo   43
    Odalisque   44
    Golliwog   44
    Carmen   46
    Merry Widow   47
    Jeune Fille—Silver Bamboo   48
    Mandarin Necklace   48
    Two-Cord Necklace: Winter Ice   49
    Two-Cord Necklace: Demimondaine   50
    Two-Cord Necklace: Bijou   52
    Three-Cord Necklace: Summer   53
    Three-Cord Necklace: Prima Donna   54

Three-Cord Necklace: Autumn 56
Batik Beads 57
The Ultimate Necklace 58

Earrings   59
Japanese Bag—*Tesage*   60
Sources for Supplies   62
Bibliography   63

Preface

Ever since the dawn of civilization, man has been stringing things on thongs so he could wear ornaments next to his body. He has also used beads in many other ways: as a means of counting prayers—the word *bead* comes from the Middle English word *bede,* meaning prayer; for adding, subtracting, and calculating—the abacus; and as symbols of rank and prestige. Coral beads have served as travelers' talismans; amber beads as healing agents; wampum or rubbed shell beads as currency and for mnemonic and symbolic purposes, depending on the arrangement of the beads on the string. Beads have even been worn as charms to ward off evil spirits. Today, however, we wear them simply because they charm us.

Beads come in a myriad sizes, shapes, and colors and in nearly as many materials; gem, stone, shell, bone, seed, pod, nut, pit, wood, metal, clay, pearl, paper, plastic, and glass are but a few.

Necklaces made of beads also come in many sizes, shapes, and colors, and again, in many materials. For the past year or more I have been exploring the limitless possibilities of design offered by beads and string: the knowledge from experimenting in this field fills the following pages. I hope my enthusiasm will be apparent. I also hope that it will prove infectious.

However, if and when the bead bug *does* bite you, be prepared for a long and virulent "affliction." Beads tend to become addictive. I know, because every morning I rise at five o'clock eager to design and string a new necklace. Fortunately, I have an outlet for my obsessive creations, for I sell most of them. But some I give to close friends, because otherwise the apartment I share with my husband and two Siamese cats would look like a series of rooms festooned with colorful strands of Spanish moss. As it is, a tie rack mounted on the inside of one closet door discreetly hides and obediently supports my personal collection of strung beads. However, here and there, now and then, an errant necklace finds its way to a handy doorknob, an empty clothes hook, a temporarily free picture nail on the wall, or a rare bare place on a horizontal plane.

The beads themselves—the loose ones—have now advanced so far and taken over for their own occupancy so much space in our home that my husband fears they plan to evict us. The little things already fill several drawers, four antique Korean hatboxes they forced me to buy to house them, a few cupboard shelves in the kitchen, and even a number of spice jars where some of them cunningly masquerade as gumdrops and others as Jordan almonds. This latest invasion of our living quarters has led me to advise anyone chatting with me while I am preparing a meal not to bite into anything found in a container with no label on it.

At the present time, my faint hope is that if I continue stringing beads at an ever more dizzying rate, I may one day conquer the horde—if only I can resist the wild urge to buy fresh masses of loose beads to replace the ones I have just strung.

But lest you be put off by what I recount here, let me assure you that, instead of suffering during my war with the invader, I have enjoyed every minute of it. I have even found it rewarding, for out of the hundreds of necklaces I have strung, four basic types, or styles, have emerged as truly successful ways of coping with the bead.

This fund of useful information I now pass on to you in book form, hoping that it will be helpful to everyone who catches "bead fever."

So turn the pages and read the prescription written out in full for those who want to survive the sickness and rout the foe. For those in a hurry, however—those in dire need of instant help—here it is in capsule form:

Rx: *String* the darned things!

Introduction

The size of a bead's hole determines to a great extent how you can use it and what kind of necklace you can make with it. If the hole is small, only one thin cord can pass through it. If the hole is not too snug, two cords may go through. If the hole is generous in size, it will accommodate three cords.

The simplest type of necklace is a pendant strung on a single string, thong, or cord knotted at the nape of the neck. A slightly more complex necklace is produced when beads with no knots between them are strung one after another on a single cord. Of course, if the cord breaks, the beads on such a necklace will scatter, and many may vanish forever. But a knot tied after each bead on the string prevents such a tragedy from happening. And although such a necklace takes a little more time to fashion, the effort is well worth your while, for the small space a knot makes between beads is attractive. Beads slightly separated one from another begin to have a bit of room in which to breathe. They assume greater importance and also seem to look more precious.

It follows, then, that lengthening the space between beads would further enhance their appeal. This is true up to a point. A good rule to follow is to string and knot, knot and string, so that an *empty space equal to the diameter of the beads you are stringing* appears between one bead and the next.

Throughout the following pages you will find that with two exceptions I have adhered to this principle. The first exception occurs when several beads are strung, one right after another, like islands on the cord. Such groups, however, are intended to be visual units. In other words, in each case I have used a variety of beads to build what should appear to be a single bead. The second exception occurs when the knotting on a three-cord necklace fills the long spaces between beads or groups of beads with a lacelike trelliswork.

(NOTE: The Chinese call these summer beads or necklaces. Beads strung close together with only a knot separating one from the next are called winter beads or necklaces.)

If you plan to string a simple single-cord necklace, you can make it more important by placing a large and ornamental bead, pendant, or tassel at its center front. Detailed instructions for making such necklaces appear on pages 17 to 19.

A greater variety of visual effects is offered to the necklace maker who decides to string on two cords instead of one. The two cords can be used as one until a double row or cluster of beads is needed. After this bit of fanfare or whimsy has been achieved, the strings may be reunited and used once again as a single cord.

To the maker of a three-cord necklace even more latitude is available, for a sculptured quality of thickness or density can be produced when the three strands separate to be strung individually before being reunited. Three cords can also be knotted to produce very decorative effects. (The Chinese have been stringing beads this way for many centuries.) The knotting in these beautiful necklaces is closely related to macramé, except that the knots we see most frequently in modern macramé are tied with four or more cords. Both types of knotting are done best on a board, with the help of pins. Detailed instructions for this kind of work appear on pages 30 through 37.

Beads with really large holes sometimes roll across one's path. They are most appealing in appearance. Naive and artless, they usually look quite primitive. And if you are lucky they may be just that, truly old, such as African, Dutch, or Russian trade beads. Only recently did I meet for the first time any of these delightful charmers. Instantly I sensed that they demanded special handling. I tried stringing and knotting them on very heavy cord. But the knots I tied offended me by their size and clumsy appearance. So I used several other approaches, and in each case was roundly defeated until at last I thought of a unique way of taming these rogues.

I made a hollow cord of fabric that I had cut into bias strips 1½″ in width. I folded the fabric lengthwise and sewed a seam ⅜″ away from the raw edges. I turned this tube right side out and strung a large-holed bead *on* it. Then I pushed a cylindrical bead *into* the fabric tube. I forced the bead along the inside of the hollow fabric cord until it hit the side of the bead strung *outside* the tube. Then I strung another of the primitive beads *on* the hollow cord. The bead inside the fabric tube kept the two large-holed beads separate, and the fabric covering the hidden cylindrical bead looked neat and tidy because it was evenly stretched over the bead it concealed.

For most of the necklaces I strung in this manner I used old sarong fabrics because of the appropriately primitive patterns to be found in antique batiks. Hence the name I gave these necklaces: Batik Beads.

(ON NEEDLE,
ABOUT 4 TIMES LENGTH)
START STRINGING WITH A LONG TAIL, SO THAT
WHEN NECKLACE IS FINISHED, KNOT 2 ENDS TOGETHER
+ THEN STRING EACH END THRU OPPISITE SIDES, AT
LEAST FOR A FEW BEADS + TRY TO MAKE ANOTHER
KNOT BETWEEN BEADS, STRING THRU MORE BEADS
THEN CUT TO FINISH.

A bead is a perforated body of glass, amber, metal, wood, etc., used as an ornament.

Materials

Attics, dresser drawers, flea markets, Salvation Army stores, and thrift and antique shops are all places where you may find good old beads. If your search turns up a necklace you really like but cannot wear because it is the wrong length, pick up your scissors and your courage and go to it: cut the cord binding those beautiful beads together. You will not be harming the beads, only freeing them so you may rearrange and restring them more to your taste.

If you cannot find the beads you need, write to the bead houses listed under Sources for Supplies.

Once you have assembled the beads you want to make into a necklace, you will need several kinds of aids.

First you must have a string, chain, thong, cord, or wire on which to thread your beads. *For knotted necklaces you should allow for the knotting, and cut a cord at least three times as long as the finished necklace will be.* For most of the necklaces I have strung, I have found that silk cord has best served my purposes. It comes from France and is available in white, which you can dye (see the next chapter) and in black. It is made in several thicknesses, or weights. It is beautiful and quite strong.

In addition, you will need a tube of Duco cement. Use it to stiffen and sharpen both ends of the silk cord so they can slip easily through a bead's bore without the help of a needle.

Colorless nail polish, nail polish remover, cotton balls, scissors, and a small ruler will also be useful.

A beading tray or a strip of corrugated cardboard can be used to facilitate the arranging of beads prior to their stringing, but neither is absolutely necessary.

The materials listed above are all you will need for a one- or two-cord necklace, plus:

- Round-nosed pliers (see page 38)

For a three-cord necklace you must add to the above a corkboard measuring at least 10″ x 15″, and a handful of 2″ long T pins. When you are ready to cut the cord *you must allow for knotting*. For Chinese knotting, cut one cord a bit longer than the finished necklace will be, and *cut two cords at least four times as long as the first cord*.

For the batik bead necklaces your needs will be as follows:

- Large-holed beads
- Smaller cylindrical beads, 6 mm. in diameter and 7 to 8 mm. in length. (These beads should have regular-sized holes.)
- Strong, thin cotton string, such as crochet thread
- A blunt, large-holed needle for threading the cotton string through the fabric tube
- Bias strips of fabric, cut 1½″ wide and about 20″ long
- Scissors, thimble, sewing needle and thread, and a "spaghetti tube" turner
- Sewing machine and steam iron
- Small metal or glass rings, squares, or ovals

mm Size Chart

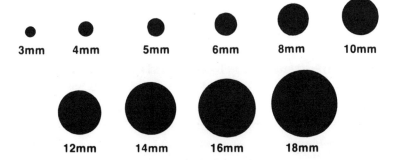

| 3mm | 4mm | 5mm | 6mm | 8mm | 10mm |

| 12mm | 14mm | 16mm | 18mm |

Tinting or Dyeing the Cord

If you want to string your beads on black cord, *buy black cord*, because it is hard to achieve a good, rich, true black color at home with Rit, Tintex, or BatiKit Cold Water Fabric Dye. With these coloring agents, however, you can tint or dye white cord to match almost any color of bead you have chosen to string.

You will need an enamel-lined cup or pot, or a small Pyrex bowl or measuring cup. *Do not mix dyes in any containers you use for eating, drinking, or cooking.*

Put a teaspoonful of dye in the cup or bowl and pour boiling water over it. Stir well.

Presoak the thread you want to tint or dye before you dip it into the hot dye bath. With a fork, stir the thread in the coloring mixture. Remove it almost immediately to check the depth of color it has reached. Wet cord is always darker than dry cord. Often I dry the cord when it seems to have reached the depth and intensity I want, only to find that it is still a bit pale. Beads strung on a matching color look best if the cord is ever so slightly darker than the beads. So when the cord needs to be a shade darker, I put it back in the dye and let it steep a few moments longer.

When the cord has been dyed to the proper tone, rinse it thoroughly in cold water. Straighten it and hang it up to dry. *Attach a weight to its two ends so it will stretch* before *you string your beads on it, not* after *the work is done.* I use a pair of heavy shears as a weight, tying the ends of the cord to the handles.

The process of dyeing cord to match beads is great fun. It should be done only during the day, and *not under artificial light.* Tint first with clear colors. Work slowly toward the tone

15

and hue you want to get. It is difficult to lighten a cord dyed too deeply, but it is easy to darken the cord.

I find it best not to mix different dyes in the same tinting bath. For example, if the cord you have dyed green is not yellow-green enough, do not add dry yellow dye to the green dye bath. Instead, prepare a yellow tint or dye and dip the rinsed green cord in it.

Gray dye, as a tint, will soften and visually age a dyed cord whose color is too raw or intense.

Gray Tintex mixed with a bit of Antique Gold Tintex produces a soft, warm greige. (Yes, here we *do* break the rule just given about mixing dyes.) Pineapple Tintex is also a very useful dye to mix with gray. But in all tinting and dyeing, experience proves to be the best teacher.

My final way of judging whether or not the cord has reached the perfect tone and color is to dry it, crush it in my hand, and lay a few beads on top of it. Only then can I tell whether or not it matches the beads. Only then can I decide whether or not it needs to be tinted one more time, made slightly bluer, redder, or more golden—or simply aged a bit.

Knots

TYPES OF KNOTS
One-Cord Knotting

You will not find it difficult to tie an Overhand Knot. Take a length of cord, make a loop in it, and put one end of the cord through the loop. Pull both ends of the cord and you have tied the knot.

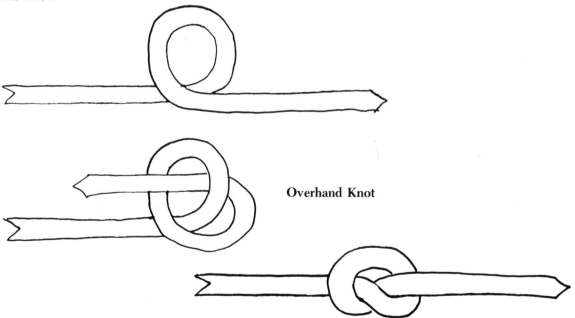

Overhand Knot

This knot can be used for all single- or double-cord necklaces. If you need a larger knot, either use a heavier cord or make your knot larger by putting the cord through the loop twice instead of once. This kind of knot (see page 18) is known as the Blood Knot.

Blood Knot

When making a simple overhand knot after stringing a bead, tie it so it fits snugly against the bead's hole. Take the cord you have just pulled through the bead, make a loop in it, and with the left hand pinch this loop between the nails of your thumb and index finger. While still exerting this pressure against the bead, slip the loop over the long cord. Pull the cord until the loop tightens and fits right up against the bead. You may find that, after slipping the loop over the long thread, your right hand should take over. Once again, the nails of the thumb and index finger will keep up the pressure of the loop against the bead while the other three fingers pull the long cord through the loop. Experiment until you can make and control with ease the placement of the knot.

The Small Turk's-Head Knot is a larger stopper knot than the overhand knot, the blood knot, or the figure-eight knot. It is not as easy to tie as the smaller knots, however, for it requires careful pulling up to achieve the neat turban look shown to the right of the diagram for the knot. But on heavy cord it can be used as a very decorative element of design.

The small Turk's-head knot may be used as a terminal knot on a necklace. It will not unravel easily.

Run the cords from the left and right sides of the necklace through the left and right sides of the joining bead. Tie the small Turk's-head knot on each side of the bead. Tie it around the necklace cord leading up to the bead. Pull each knot into shape *close* to the bead. Put a small drop of cement in each knot where the end of the cord has emerged. Let the cement dry. Then, with side-clipping pliers, snip off the excess cord, right up against the knot.

The Lark's Head, or Cow Hitch Knot, may be used when you want to attach a pierced ornament to the center front of a necklace. Double the cord. Hold its two free ends in one hand. Push the looped end through the ornament's hole, then put the two free ends of the cord through the loop and pull them tight. This knot can also be used to hold together the centers of several short lengths of beaded cord you have strung to make a tassel.

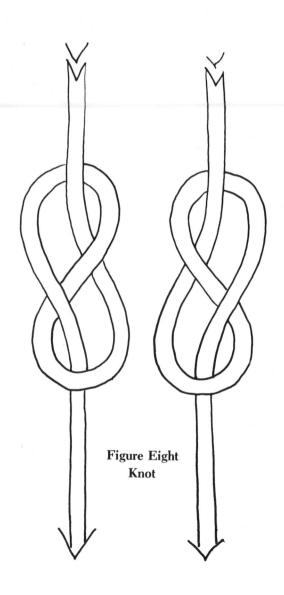

Figure Eight Knot

Small Turk's-Head Knot

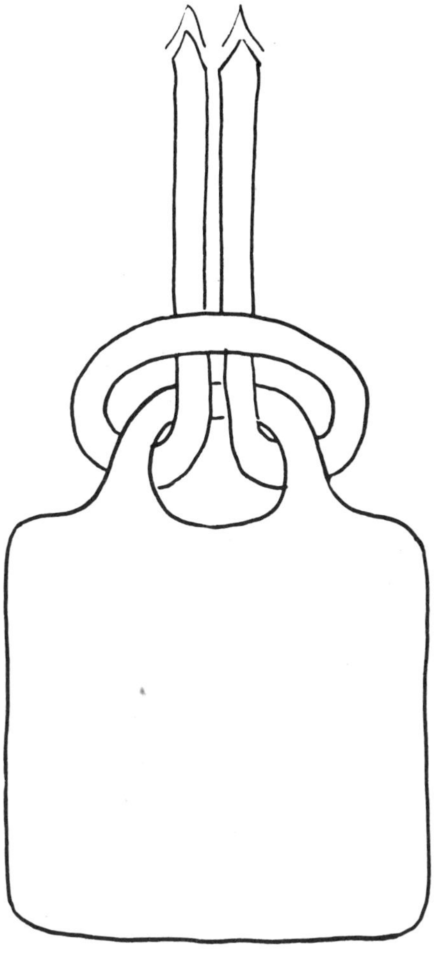

Lark's-Head
(Cow Hitch) Knot

Two-Cord Knotting

The Carrick Bend, similar to the Bosun's Whistle, can be used just above a pendant.

Tie the knot carefully and pull it into its interwoven ring wherever it wants to shape up on the double cords of your necklace. Then move it toward the desired position in your design by pulling one cord at a time through its pattern in the knot. Use the small round-nosed pliers for this process. When the knot has been relocated, tighten it carefully. Again, the small pliers will be most helpful. (See page 38.)

**Single Tatted Chain Knot
(Seesaw Knot)**

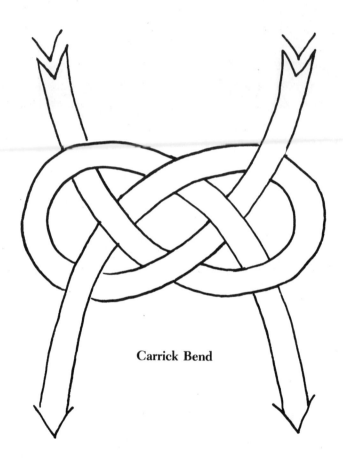

Carrick Bend

The Single Tatted Chain, or Seesaw Knot, is made with two cords. It produces a neat, firm, braidlike effect. It is *very* easy to work. I would have liked to call it Idiot's Delight, but another, similar knotted chain bears that charming name.

Take two cords and tie a temporary knot to join them together. Pass the working ends of the cords through a bead. Anchor the bead to a board by using four **T** pins to make a skeletal wigwam over the bead.

Now pull the left cord toward you. Take the right cord and make a half hitch over the left cord, as shown at the top of the diagram for the knot. Pull the right cord back up against the bead. Then pull the right cord toward you. Take the left cord and make a half hitch over the right cord. Pull the left cord up against the half hitch just made. Continue knotting in this manner. Exert an even tension while knotting, and work with a flowing rhythm. This will produce a smooth "braid." Count the knots as you work. Use an even number of half hitches. Always begin your work with the cord on the right side, unless you are left-handed and prefer always to start your work with the cord on the left.

Each time you stop knotting in order to string a bead on the two cords, make sure that the right cord remains on the right and the left cord remains on the left.

Use cord that is heavy enough, when knotted, to keep the beads from slipping on the finished necklace. When you have finished knotting the "braid," you may improve its appearance by holding it over a kettle's steaming spout. This will set the knots. The "braid" will become more supple and the necklace will therefore hang with more grace.

The Chinese use the Bosun's Whistle Knot before and after each butterfly knot (shown completed on page 27) because it stabilizes the larger knot. In addition, it is aesthetically pleasing to see the flat, looped butterfly between the neat, round bosun's whistle knots.

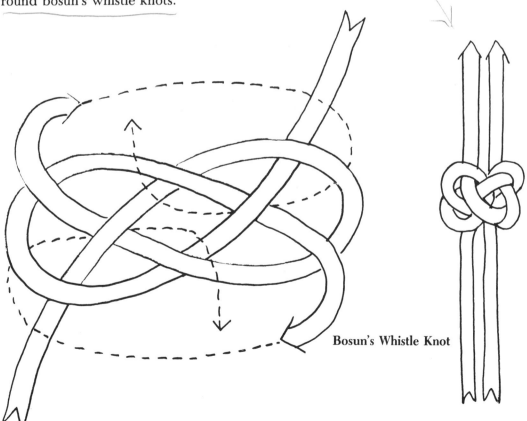

Bosun's Whistle Knot

The accompanying diagram illustrates tying the bosun's whistle knot over two cords. The knot may be used where a terminal knot may be required at the back of the neck after the two left-side cords have gone through the last bead and the right-side cords have gone through the same bead in the opposite direction. The knot is then tied over the two cords and worked into shape tight against the bead. You must clip the excess cords *close* to the knot.

The knot may also be used to attach two cords to a ring or a pendant. Again, clip the excess cord tight up against the knot.

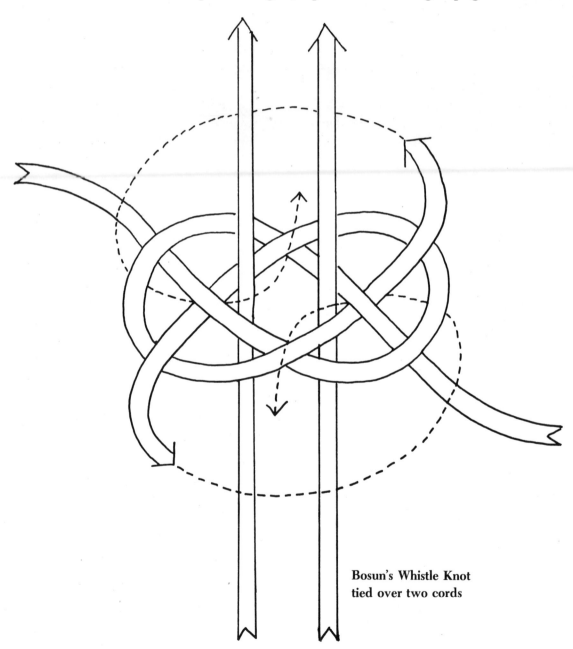

**Bosun's Whistle Knot
tied over two cords**

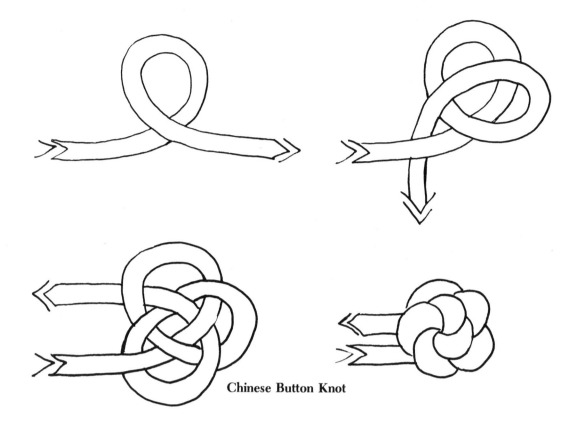

Chinese Button Knot

The Chinese button knot may be used as the stopper knot at the bottom of a large bead to make the bead a pendant bead.

Pin arrangement for weaving the Chinese Butterfly, or Eternal Knot.

When the two cords have been properly interwoven, following diagrams 1, 2, 3, and 4, remove all but six of the pin guides. There should be one in each of the six outer loops in the border of the knot. Now, pull up the pin in loop A. Keeping it in the loop, move it up next to the beginning of the knot and push it into the board again. Move the pin in loop B up close to the first pin while still keeping it in the loop. Move the pin in loop C up close to pin B. Then move the pins in loops D, E, and F up close to the beginning of the knot. See the diagram for the final diamond-shaped placement of the pins.

Take a pair of round-nosed pliers. (See page 38.) Pull loop A in the direction indicated by the arrow. Then pull loop B until loop A hugs its pin. Pull loop C until loop B hugs its pin. Pull cord D at the bottom of the knot until loop C hugs its pin.

(A blunt needlepoint needle slipped into the small loop opposite each large loop will make the pulling up of the knot a very simple process.)

Follow the same manner of pulling loops E, F, and G until the knot is in a fairly neat and flat shape.

Remove the pins from the board and take the knot in your hand. Use the small round-nosed pliers to tighten the knot further. Follow the loop sequence given above. When pulled into its final shape the knot should look like the diagram on page 27.

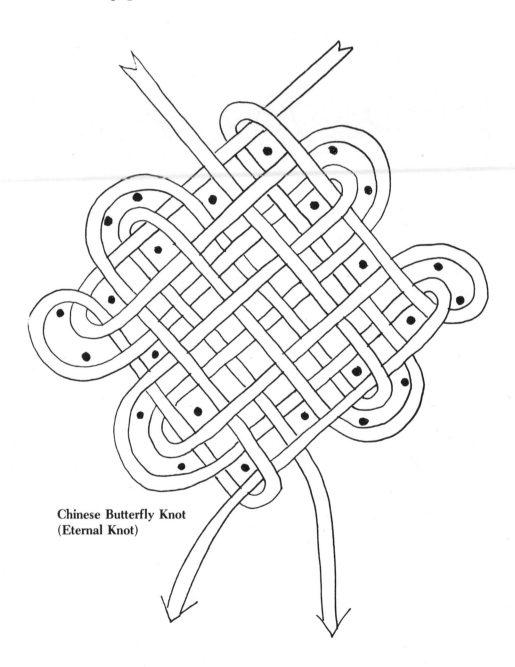

Chinese Butterfly Knot
(Eternal Knot)

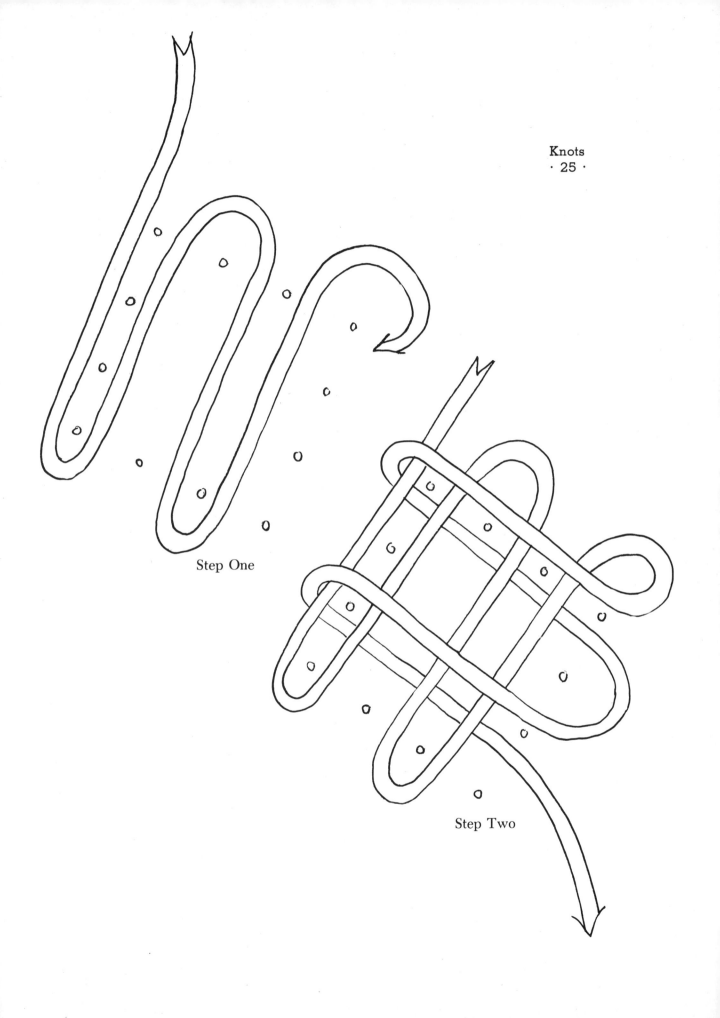

Step One

Step Two

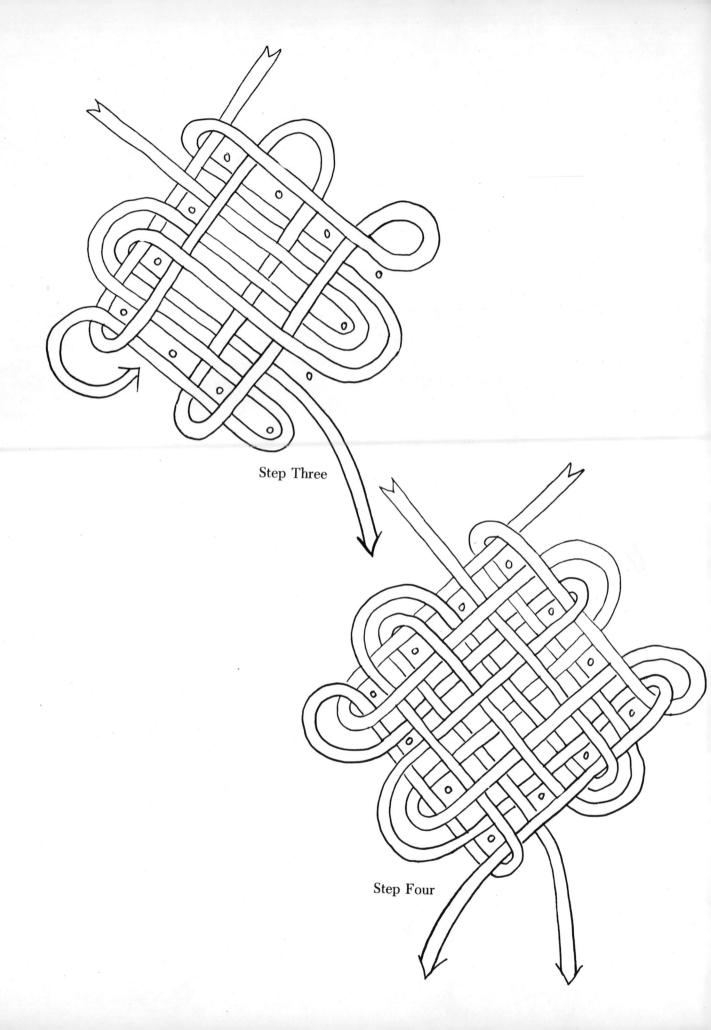

Step Three

Step Four

Step Five

The Half Knot is made with two cords. It is the first step we take when we tie shoelaces. It can be a left-handed or a right-handed knot, i.e., left cord over right, or right over left.

To tie a Square Knot, or Reef Knot, the half knot is repeated once. But if the first half knot is left-handed, the second half knot must be right-handed.

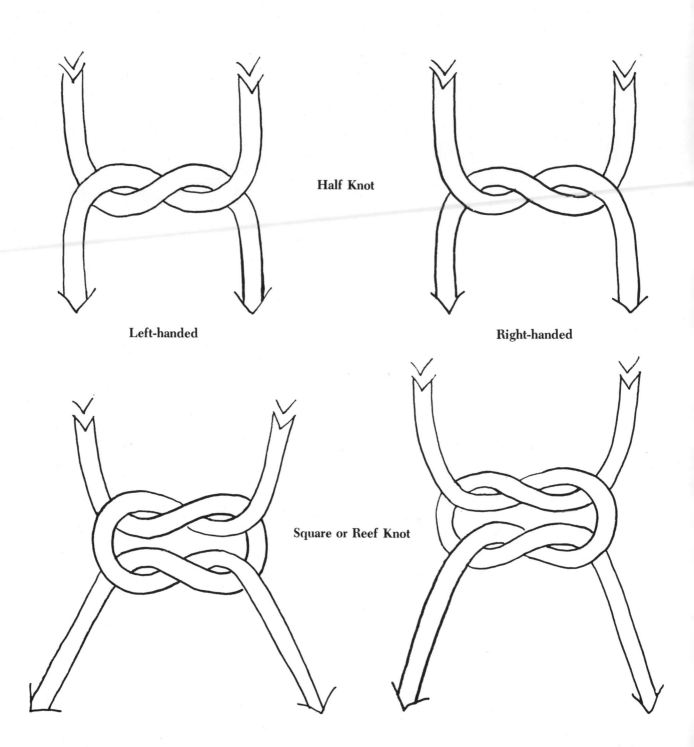

Half Knot

Left-handed   Right-handed

Square or Reef Knot

A left-handed half knot followed by another left-handed half knot will produce the Granny Knot—as will a right-handed half knot followed by another right-handed half knot.

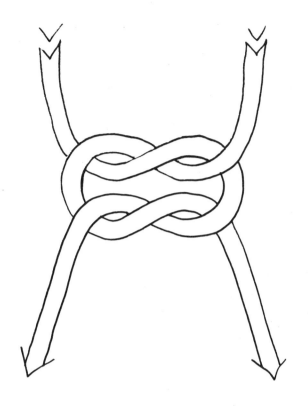

Granny Knots

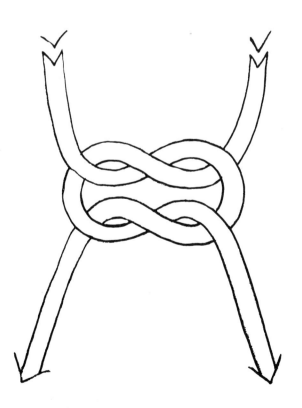

Three-Cord Knotting

A necklace made with three-cord knotting can be done successfully only if it is worked on a board. Cork is the best material on which to work, since T pins must be pressed into it to keep the cords in place. Two-inch pins are suitable for the purpose.

The center cord for the three-cord necklace need not be much longer than the finished necklace will be, for it is only the core. You tie the other two cords over it, so they must be at least three times as long as the length of the center cord, in order to allow for knotting.

Begin any three-cord knotted necklace at the center. Whether the necklace is tied off at center front or finishes at the back will determine where you begin working.

At the top of the board, pin the centers of the three cords to the surface, an inch separating each one from the next. Use T pins. Do not pierce the cord, but tie the cords to the pins with a lark's-head knot or any kind of easily untied knot or winding process you prefer to use.

Fix the lower end of the center cord to the bottom of the board. This cord will be a core, and will for the most part remain taut, while you use the other two cords to tie Solomon knots upon it. It will be loosened at its lower end only when its working end must pass through a bead's hole.

For purposes of identification I will hereafter refer to the three cords as C for the center, or core cord, L for the cord on the left, and R for the cord on the right.

At the top of the board, slightly below the place where the three cords have been attached to the three T pins, press two T pins into the cork, one between L and C, and a second one, parallel to the first, between C and R. Your first knot will be tied and pulled up against these two pins.

The board and three cords are now ready for you to begin tying knots.

Take up cord R. Pass its working end *under* the taut C cord and *over* the upper end of cord L. Then take the lower end of cord L and pass its working end *over* the C cord and *under* the upper end of cord R. Pull the ends of L and R until the half knot you have just tied slips up against the two pins near the top of the board. Then tie the second half knot necessary to make one Solomon knot: take R (which for the moment lies to the left of C) and pass its working end under C and *over* the upper end of L (which for the moment lies to the right of C). Then take L and pass its working end *over* C and under the upper end of R. Pull the ends of L and R until the second half knot slips up against the first half knot. You have now tied a square knot. However, it has the C cord as a core, or spine, incorporated in it.

Push two **T** pins into the corkboard immediately below the Solomon knot, one between L and C, and one between C and R. Use a six-inch ruler and measure the space you want to leave open in the pattern of knots and spaces you are following. Push another two **T** pins into the corkboard where you want the open space to end and the next knot to begin. Tie your second knot, following the method used for the first knot.

Continue knotting and spacing in this manner until you need to add a bead to the necklace.

Release the lower end of C. Put the working ends of L, C, and R through the bead's hole. Push the bead up against the last knot you have tied.

Take C—*and make sure it is C, and not L or R*—(it will be the shortest cord of the three) and reattach it to the bottom end of the corkboard.

Continue knotting, spacing, and beading until you have completed half of the necklace.

Release the three cords where they have been attached at the top of the board. Turn the necklace around so that the unworked cords for the second half of the necklace lie across the board from top to bottom. Attach the center of the necklace to the board again and work the second half of the necklace.

For this half, reverse the tying process. Where the first part of the necklace was tied with R over L, then L over R for each Solomon knot, tie the second part of the necklace with L over R and R over L to make each Solomon knot. Otherwise, when you remove the necklace from the board, it will make a half twist at its center.

Finish the necklace with either a center front tassel or tassels, using the "locking" bead's hole either vertically or horizontally. Pass the six cords—three from each side—through the bead's hole and string each separately to form a six-strand tassel or two three-strand tassels.

If the necklace is to be tied at the back of the neck, work a flat sinnit band on each side, then tie off each of the three cords on each side and end each cord with a decorative bead, then an overhand knot, as shown in the diagrams starting on page 32.

Use Duco cement to seal the overhand knots at the end of each strand.

If you want to make the necklace lie flat, take it to the

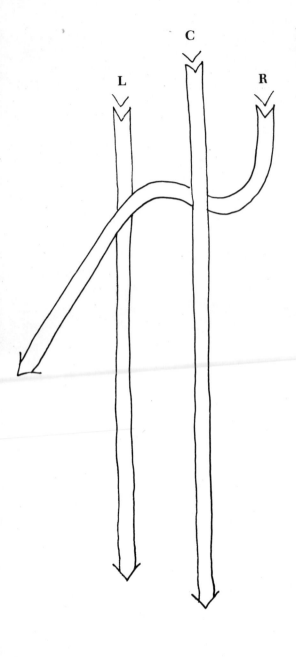

kitchen. Put a kettle of water over a fire. When it comes to a boil, take the necklace, pull it taut from end to end, and, holding it a few inches away from the kettle's steaming spout, move it back and forth through the steam. This will set the knots in place and make the necklace look much better than it did when you first removed it from the corkboard. AVOID STEAMING THE BEADS—THEY MAY CRACK.

From here on, in tying three-strand necklaces, follow even-numbered pages for the left side of a necklace and odd-numbered pages for the right side. Lower diagrams show the knot pulled together.

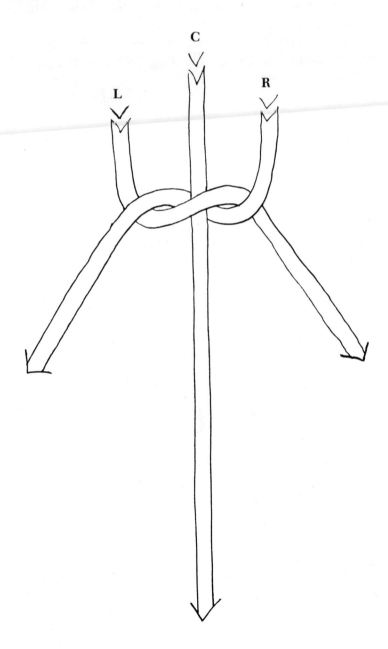

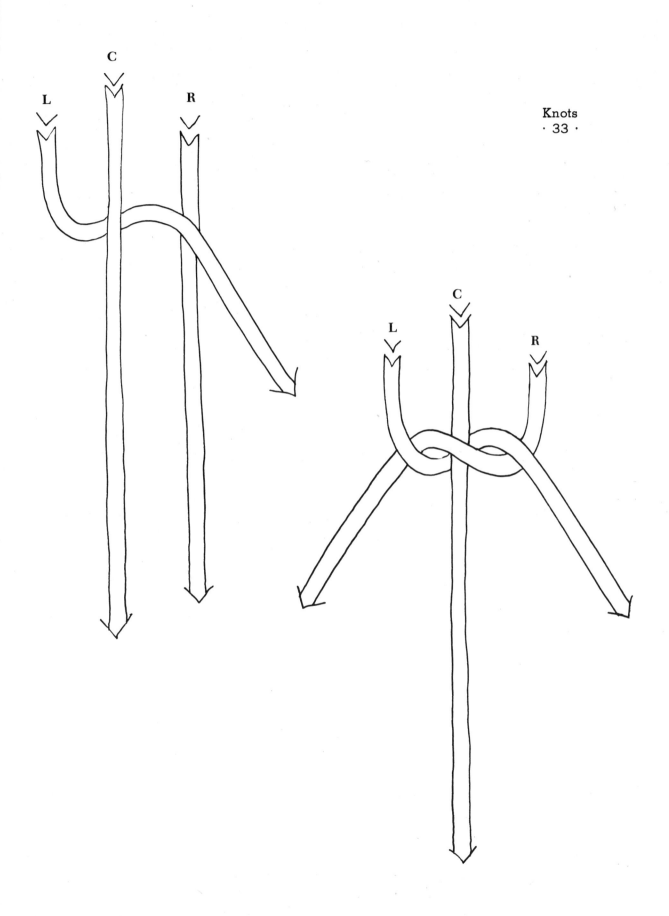

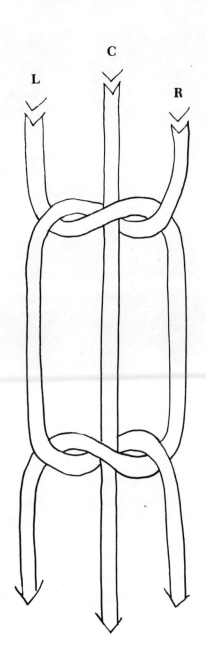

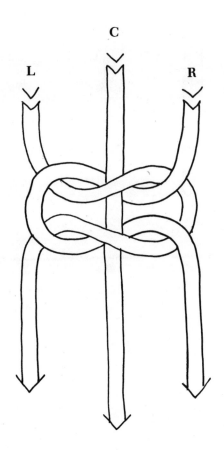

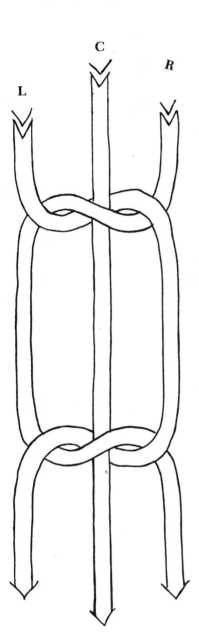

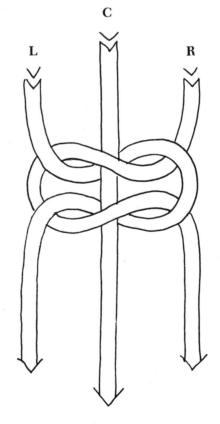

When the square knot, or reef knot, is tied over a central cord the result is the Solomon knot, the one used in Chinese three-cord knotting. The Solomon knot, repeated, knot after knot, will produce a flat, ribbonlike strip, or band, of knotting called a Flat Sinnit, or a Portuguese Square Sinnit.

See left for a *left-handed* Flat Sinnit or Portuguese Square Sinnit.

See right for a *right-handed* Flat Sinnit or Portuguese Square Knot.

Flat Sinnit Knot, Left
(Portuguese Square Sinnit)

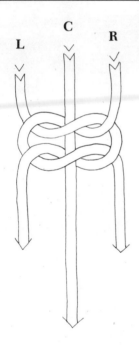

A Twisting Sinnit, also known as the Portuguese Spiral Sinnit, is produced by tying a left-handed half knot, then repeating this knot over and over.

Twisting Sinnit, Left
(Portuguese Spiral Sinnit)

**Flat Sinnit Knot, Right
(Portuguese Square Sinnit)**

The right-handed half knot repeated over and over will produce a sinnit that twists in the direction opposite to the twist of the sinnit tied with left-handed half knots.

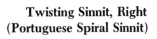

**Twisting Sinnit, Right
(Portuguese Spiral Sinnit)**

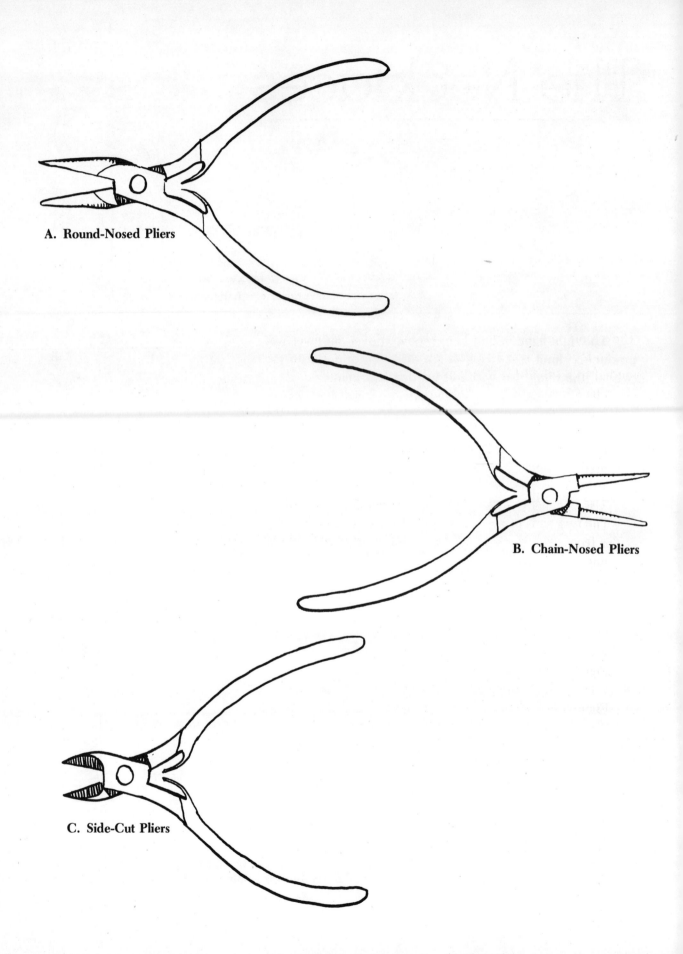

A. Round-Nosed Pliers

B. Chain-Nosed Pliers

C. Side-Cut Pliers

The Necklaces

The accompanying figures provide patterns of stringing for you to follow or adapt to your own needs. They are not intended to be rigid formats that you may not change.

I have drawn them on graph paper on which every heavy line represents an inch so that you may see how long the original necklaces are. You may want to make a shorter necklace than many of the long ones illustrated here, so find the length that looks best on you. To do so, measure a necklace you often wear, one whose length you like and is flattering to you. Use this measurement when making your first necklace.

The two ends of every necklace must be joined either at center front or at the nape of the neck. In either case, begin stringing your necklace in the middle of the cord, halfway between its two ends.

Figures 1 through 9 are single-cord necklaces whose ends join at the nape of the neck.

Figures 10 and 11 are single-cord necklaces whose ends join at center front.

Figures 12 and 13 are double-cord necklaces whose ends join at the nape of the neck.

Figures 14 and 15 are short triple-cord necklaces whose ends finish and tie at the nape of the neck.

Figures 16 and 17 are each of long triple-cord necklaces whose ends finish in a tassel at center front.

Figure 18 is a pattern for batik beads.

Figure 19, "The Ultimate Necklace," features the Chinese butterfly knot.

Figure 20 illustrates earrings.

Figures 21 and 22 are patterns for a Japanese bag, or *tesage*.

To make necklace closings using a spring ring or any other type of metal fastener follow these steps:

Put one end of the necklace cord through the eye of one part of the fastening device. Turn the cord back on itself. Take a heavy cotton thread—buttonhole and carpet thread or glacé thread. Lay this along the cord where it is double, as shown in Figure A of the accompanying illustrations for whipping. Loop the thread near the eye of the fastening. Turn the whipping thread back on itself and begin to bind the necklace cord where it is double. Whip neatly and tightly *toward* the fastening device. Then put the working end of the whipping thread through its own loop. Pull the two free ends of the whipping thread until both looped ends are concealed under the whipping, as shown in Figure B. Trim the exposed ends of the whipping thread. The whipped joining will then look like Figure C. Finally, trim the excess of the necklace cord. The finished whipping should be no thicker than the cord when it is single. For purposes of clarity, the illustration shows the finished whipping twice as wide or thick—as it should be.

If you want to add strength to the whipping, put a drop of Duco cement on it and twirl the bound section between the tips of your thumb and forefinger.

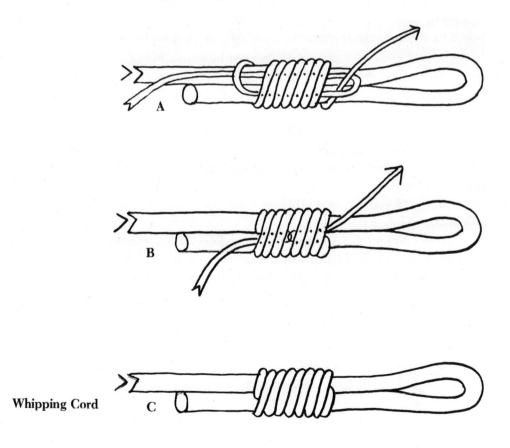

Whipping Cord

"NECKLACE" NECKLACE (single strand, with no pendants or tassels)

FIGURE 1.   7 frosted light amethyst beads, 14 mm. in size

14 clear medium blue melon beads, 6 mm. in size

23 clear amethyst round beads, 10 mm. in size

28 ornamental metal caps. (These separate the 14-mm. beads from the 6-mm. beads, i.e., 4 caps for each grouping.)

46 cup caps. (Each round 10-mm. bead has a 4-mm. brass cup cap at each end.)

Strung and knotted on silk cord dyed to match the 10-mm. amethyst beads.

Begin the necklace at the center front. Make an overhand knot. String a 6-mm. melon bead, an ornamental cap (cup toward the bead), another ornamental cap (cup away from the bead), a large frosted amethyst bead, a cap (cup toward the large bead), another cap (cup away from the large bead), a small melon bead, and then make an overhand knot pulled tightly against the group of beads just strung. Allow ⅜″ of cord to show before making the next overhand knot. String on a cap, a round amethyst bead, a cap, and then tie an overhand knot pulled tightly against the group of cap, bead, and cap. String two more spaced groups of cap, bead, and cap, as shown on the diagram. Then repeat the pattern of beads used in the center front and described above.

Continue stringing and knotting until the necklace is half as long as you want it to be. Then work the other half of the necklace.

Before joining the two ends of the necklace at the back, tie an overhand knot on each end, ⅜″ away from the last group of beads on each side of the necklace. String a cap, a bead, and a cap on one end of the necklace. Then insert the cord of the other end of the necklace through the same cap, bead, and cap, but insert this cord from the opposite end of the group, thus closing the circle of the necklace. Knot each cord with an overhand knot pulled tightly against the closing group of cap, bead, and cap. Make an ornamental tassel of cap, bead, and cap, as shown on the diagram. Tie a figure-eight knot to hold each tassel group in place. Apply a drop of Duco cement to each final knot. Press the cement into the knot. Let dry, and then cut off the excess cord, snipping it *close* to the final knot. Then apply another drop of cement to each knot to seal the cut cord.

FIGURE 1

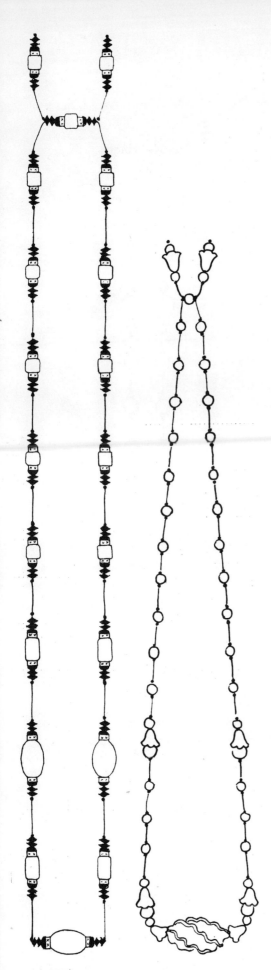

ANASTASIA

FIGURE 2.   3 important clear and frosted carved beads, 15 x 24 mm. in size

4 rectangular beads, clear colorless glass, 9 x 15 mm. in size

13 cubes, clear colorless glass, 9 x 9 x 9 mm. in size

80 black jet diamond-shaped rondelles, 5 mm. in size

40 round jet beads, 5 mm. in size

40 rhinestone rondelles, crystal set in black, 5 mm. in size

Strung and knotted on black silk cord.

Each group of beads on the necklace is strung as follows: Two black jet diamond-shaped rondelles, a round jet bead, a rhinestone rondelle, a glass bead, a rhinestone rondelle, a round jet bead, and two black jet diamond-shaped rondelles. An overhand knot at the beginning and end of each group holds it in place on the necklace and separates group from group.

Follow Figure 2 for the placement of the glass beads. The detailed instructions given for the Necklace necklace (Figure 1) should be followed, except that the distance between groups of beads on Figure 2 measures ⅝″, so allow ⅝″ between overhand knots when making a necklace to resemble the one in Figure 2.

SPRING

FIGURE 3.   1 large cranberry-colored Venetian glass bead, fluted, 22 x 36 mm.

6 frosted colorless bell beads

4 cranberry-colored 8 mm. beads

39 frosted colorless 6 mm. beads

Strung and knotted on cranberry silk cord.

Follow the general instructions given for the Necklace necklace, Figure 1.

FIGURE 2   FIGURE 3

GYPSY

FIGURE 4.   1 carved amber tortoiseshell cylinder bead,
                15 x 24 mm. in size
            2 amber tortoiseshell cones
            4 amber tortoiseshell round beads, 9 mm. in
                size
            2 amber tortoiseshell round beads, 12 mm. in
                size
            5 amber tortoiseshell cylinder beads, 6 x 12 mm.
                in size
            54 amber tortoiseshell round beads, 5 mm. in
                size
            24 rhinestone and jet rondelles, 6 mm. in size

Strung and knotted on black silk cord.

Follow the general instructions given for the Necklace
necklace, Figure 1.

PENDANT NECKLACE IN SILVER BAMBOO

FIGURE 5.   2″ long pendant
            24 clear glass beads, 8 mm. in size
            4 textured silver beads, 12 mm. in size
            48 silver gearlike rondelles, 6 mm. in size; guard
                the clear glass beads
            8 ornamental silver caps for the textured silver
                beads
            For each space between beads on the neck-
                lace I have used three ¼″ "liquid silver" tube
                beads and four 2-mm. silver beads to make
                what I call "silver bamboo."

Strung with no knots on silver gray silk cord.

Make a lark's-head or cow hitch knot to attach the center
of a long cord to the ring or hole on a pendant. String a small
silver bead, a gearlike rondelle, a clear glass bead, a gearlike
rondelle, and a small silver bead on both cords, using them as
one. Separate the two cords and tie an overhand knot on each
cord *close* to the beads just strung.

Then, without knotting, string each side of the necklace,
following the pattern of Figure 5.

For closing the necklace follow the instructions given for
the Necklace necklace, Figure 1.

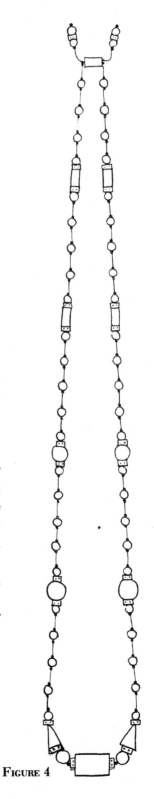

FIGURE 4   FIGURE 5

ODALISQUE

FIGURE 6. 1 large fluted topaz melon bead, 16 mm. in size
1 topaz cut-crystal teardrop with lengthwise hole, 20 x 8 mm. at its widest part
7 gray cut-crystal beads, 8 mm. in size
54 topaz cut-crystal beads, 5 mm. in size
10 gray cut-crystal diamond-shaped rondelles
1 topaz cut-crystal diamond-shaped rondelle, at the tip of the teardrop
2 rhinestone rondelles set in black, 7 mm. in size
18 rhinestone rondelles set in black, 6 mm. in size
4 smooth topaz teardrops in pendant part

Strung and knotted on black silk cord.

Begin this necklace at the center front. String a small bead as a "stopper" for the bottom of the teardrop. Then take both ends of the cord and use them together, as one, to string the teardrop and rhinestone pendant part of the necklace. Tie an overhand knot at the top of the pendant. Separate the cords. String each of the two arms above the pendant. (They look like the arms of a Y.) Tie an overhand knot at the end of each arm. Take the cord on the right side and string, from the right, the five beads forming the bar across the center front of the necklace. Then take the cord on the left and string the same beads, entering from the left side. Pull the two cords taut and tie an overhand knot on each one, close to the five-bead bar. Then string the rest of the necklace following the pattern of beads and spaces shown in Figure 6.

For closing the necklace, follow the instructions given for the Necklace necklace, Figure 1.

GOLLIWOG

FIGURE 7. 3 white "tile" beads with large holes. These are tubular and measure 6 x 6 mm.
1 large white tube bead above the tassel
6 shiny black prunelike beads, 14 mm. in size
20 white porcelain beads, shiny ovals, 8 x 14 mm. in size

FIGURE 6

16 round jet beads, 5 mm. in size
1 jet diamond-shaped bead above the tassel
As many black and white diamond-shaped
rondelles as you need to make a 6- or 8-strand
tassel

Strung and knotted on black silk cord.

Begin this necklace at center front. But first, make the tassel:

String three or four lengths of black and white diamond-shaped rondelles. Begin each strand with an overhand knot and a 5-mm. jet bead. Separate the first half of the strand from the second half of it by tying two overhand knots with a small space between them, as shown on the tassel detail in Figure 7. End each strand with a 5-mm. bead and an overhand knot. Seal the end knots with Duco cement before snipping off the excess cord, *close* to each end knot. Then seal the knots again with another drop of Duco cement.

Take the long cord for the main part of the necklace and fold it in half. Across this center fold, which will be at the center front of the necklace, hang the three or four strands of the tassel. The small space at the center of each tassel strand should fold over the center of the necklace cord.

Take the two ends of the necklace cord and use them as one to string the group of three beads directly above the tassel (the foot of the **Y** part of the necklace). Pull the tassel tightly up against the first bead and then tie an overhand knot *close* to the third bead of the group.

Separate the two ends of the necklace cord and string each one (the arms of the **Y**), three jet beads on each arm.

Take the cord on the right side and, from the right, string the three beads, forming the bar across the center front of the necklace. Then take the cord on the left side and string the same group of beads, entering from the left side. Pull the two cords tight, string a black bead on each, and tie an overhand knot *close* to each black bead. Then string each side of the necklace, following the pattern of beads and spaces shown in Figure 7.

For closing the necklace, follow the instructions given for the Necklace necklace, Figure 1.

FIGURE 7A

FIGURE 7

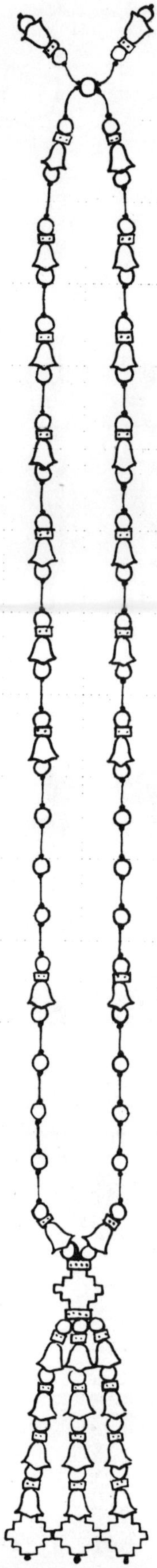

CARMEN

FIGURE 8

FIGURE 8.　　7 large lime green stepped beads, 18 mm. in size

2 rhinestone rondelles set in black, 8 mm. in size

44 rhinestone rondelles set in black, 6 mm. in size

44 frosted crystal bell beads

77 lime green round beads, 6 mm. in size

Strung and knotted on black silk cord.

Begin this necklace at center front.

Make a tassel. Follow the method shown in Figure 7, but follow the bead placement shown in Figure 8, i.e., make three strands with a space in the center of each strand. (When they are caught up by the necklace cord they will hang as a six-strand tassel.)

Take the necklace cord and double it. Make a loose lark's-head loop with the center front of the necklace cord. Slip the three tassel strands through the loop and arrange them so the space at the center of each strand lies on the necklace cord. Tighten the lark's-head hitch to hold the three strands of the tassel in place. Take the two ends of the necklace cord and, using them temporarily as one, pass them through the first rhinestone rondelle, the stepped bead, and the second rhinestone rondelle. This group of three beads hangs at the center front of the necklace. Pull the tassel up tight against the rhinestone rondelle at the bottom of the group and tie an overhand knot tight against the rhinestone rondelle at the top of the group.

Separate the two strands of the necklace. String the left side of the necklace, then the right, following the pattern of beads and spaces shown in the diagram.

Join the two sides of the necklace at center back, following the instructions given for the Necklace necklace, Figure 1.

MERRY WIDOW

FIGURE 9.   1 fancy cut-crystal bead, clear and frosted,
              16 mm. in size
           8 dull black beads, 6 mm. in size
           16 dull black bugle beads
           76 dull black beads, 4 mm. in size
           1 dull black wafer rondelle, 8 mm. in size
           2 crystal rhinestone rondelles, 10 mm. in size
           44 crystal rhinestone rondelles, 5 mm. in size
           9 frosted crystal beads, graduated, 6 mm. at
              the nape of the neck to 12 mm. at the front
              of the necklace

Strung and knotted on black silk cord.

Begin this necklace at center front.

Make a tassel. Follow the method shown in Figure 7, but follow the placement of beads shown in Figure 9, i.e., make four strands with a space in the center of each strand. (When they are caught up in the necklace cord they will hang as an eight-strand tassel.)

Take the necklace cord and attach the four tassel strands —at their centers—with a lark's-head or cow hitch knot. Take the two ends of the necklace cord and, using them temporarily as one, pass them through the first rhinestone rondelle, the large crystal bead, the second rhinestone rondelle, and the black wafer rondelle. This group of four beads hangs at the center front of the necklace.

Pull the eight-strand tassel up tight against the first rhinestone rondelle, and tie an overhand knot *close* to the black wafer rondelle at the top of the group.

Separate the two strands of the necklace. String the left side of the necklace, then the right, following the pattern of beads and spaces shown in the diagram.

Join the two sides of the necklace at center back, following the instructions given for the Necklace necklace, Figure 1.

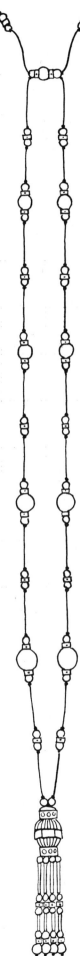

FIGURE 9

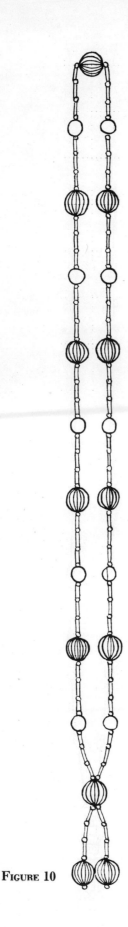

FIGURE 10

JEUNE FILLE—SILVER BAMBOO

FIGURE 10.   2 frosted crystal melon beads, 12 mm. in size,
in front "tie"
10 silver melon beads, 12 mm. in size
10 frosted crystal round beads, 8 mm. in size
The beads are separated by three ¼" "liquid
silver" tubes and four silver beads, 3 mm.
in size

*Strung on silver gray silk cord. Knotted only in the front
of the necklace, below the "tie."*

Begin this necklace at center back and string each side
down to the center front, following the pattern of bead placement shown in the diagram.

No knots are used in this necklace except at the end of
each of the two ornamental strands of beads hanging below
the bead at the center front. This bead is used as the "joining"
bead. The left and right cords go through it together, i.e., in the
same direction—and then separate below it to make the ornamental ends of the necklace.

MANDARIN NECKLACE

FIGURE 11.   9 carnelian melon beads or any important bead,
14 mm. in size
18 clear crystal round beads, 8 mm. in size
10 clear crystal round beads, 4 mm. in size
12 clear crystal round beads, 6 mm. in size
Opaque dull black wafer rondelles 6 mm. in size;
fill the long spaces between each melon bead
and its two glass guard beads

*Strung and knotted on carnelian-colored silk cord. (The knots
are tied before and after each melon bead, and not
between the glass beads and the wafer rondelles.)*

*It is very important to stretch the cord before making this
kind of necklace.*

Begin this necklace at center back. Make an overhand
knot. String an 8-mm. bead. Then string as many black wafer
rondelles as needed to cover a little more than three inches of
cord. (Remember this count and use it for all groups of wafer
rondelles in the necklace.) String on another 8-mm. bead. Tie
an overhand knot *close* to the second 1-mm. bead. String a 14-
mm. melon bead. Tie an overhand knot. Then repeat the 8-
mm. bead, wafer rondelles, and 8-mm. bead pattern. Tie an

overhand knot. String another 14-mm. bead, tie a knot, etc.

At center front, tie an overhand knot on the right and left cords. The right cord then goes through the center front melon bead from the right to the left. The left cord goes through the same melon bead from the left to the right. Pull each cord tight and tie an overhand knot on each cord, *close* to the melon bead. String four small beads on each cord. Then join the two cords and string them as one through three wafer beads and a small crystal bead. The cords then separate again and are strung independently to hang as the pair of ornamental ends at the bottom of the necklace.

Seal the knots ending these two strands with Duco cement, as described in detail in the instructions given for the Necklace necklace, Figure 1.

NOTE: This necklace works up beautifully if you use sequins instead of wafer rondelles for the long stretches of beads. If you want to use sequins, *do not* take them off the thread they are already strung on when you buy them. Lay about three inches at the end of your cord on top of three inches at the end of the thread on which the sequins are strung, and slip the sequins from the thread onto your cord. It would be much too time consuming to count the sequins. It is easier to measure the length of the group you want to transfer from their thread to yours. Either put a small paper clip at the end of this bunch before transferring them to your cord, or measure the transferred sequins as their number increases on your cord.

TWO-CORD NECKLACE: Winter Ice

The original necklace was made of clear, colorless glass beads.

FIGURE 12.   1 Deco bead at center front
48 drop beads
1 tube bead, 8 x 12 mm. in size
4 tube beads, 6 x 26 mm. in size
1 tube bead, 6 x 12 mm. in size
4 diamond-shaped double cone beads, 12 mm. across and 12 mm. from end to end
24 round beads, 6 mm. in size

Strung and knotted on double black silk cord.

Begin this necklace at center front.
Use two thin cords. They will be strung as one except

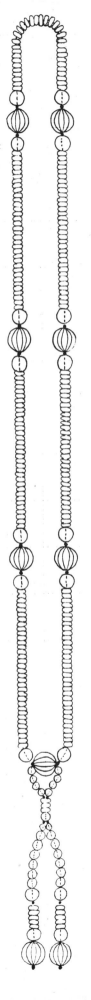

FIGURE 11

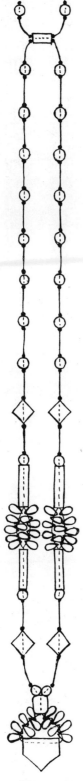

FIGURE 12

where they emerge from the horizontally strung bead at center front, and once on each side of the necklace about four inches above the center front bead.

Put the two cords through the center front bead. String each strand of the two strands emerging *on the right* of the center front bead with six drop beads. String each strand of the two strands emerging *on the left* of the center front bead with six drop beads. Join all four strands—for so they seem to be now—and use them as one while you string the center "joining" bead. Then separate the four cords into two pairs. String the right pair through a small bead. String the left pair through a small bead. Now pull each pair of cords tight. Adjust the drop beads below the joining bead so they nestle comfortably. Then tie an overhand knot with the pair of cords on the right side, close to the small bead. Tie an overhand knot with the pair of cords on the left side, *close* to the small bead.

Use the pair of cords on the right as one. Knot, bead, and knot following the pattern of beads and spaces shown on the diagram. The cords separate only once on the right side when they emerge from the long tube bead. At this point you string six drop beads on each cord, then join them together again and use them once more as one cord.

Use the pair of cords on the left as one. Knot, bead, and knot following the pattern of beads and spaces you have used for stringing the pair of cords on the right.

Finish the necklace at center back, following the instructions given for the Necklace necklace, Figure 1.

TWO-CQRD NECKLACE: Demimondaine

FIGURE 13. 150 lime green iridescent bugle beads
178 cut-crystal rondelles, morion color, 6 mm. in size
28 frosted amethyst bell beads
24 frosted amethyst flower beads
2 cut-crystal beads, morion color, 6 mm. in size

Strung on black silk cord.

Begin this necklace at center front.

Make two tassels, i.e., string six lengths of beads, three for the left side and three for the right. Follow the instructions given with Figure 7.

Take the two long cords to be used for the necklace and fold each in half. Make a lark's-head or cow hitch knot at the fold of each strand and use each hitch as a sling for a tassel. See the detailed drawing (Fig. 13A) of the method of hanging the two tassels from the center front bead on this necklace. The drawing shows only one strand of tassel hanging from each lark's-head loop. It shows the bell bead on each side ready to slip down to cover the lark's-head loop. It shows the cords from each side as they go through the center front bead's cord. The bead is shown as though cut in half so that the cords' passage through its core is visible. *Note:* The detail does not show an overhand knot above each bell bead. *Be sure* to tie an overhand knot *close* to the top of each bell bead after it has been pushed hard against the lark's-head loop holding the tassel.

The two cords on the right will be used as one until they are separated about halfway up the necklace. Then they are strung independently. They cross back and forth through the flower beads that look like steps on a ladder.

The two cords on the left will also be used as one. String them in the same manner as you have strung the beads on the right side.

Close the necklace at center back, following the directions given for the Necklace necklace, Figure 1.

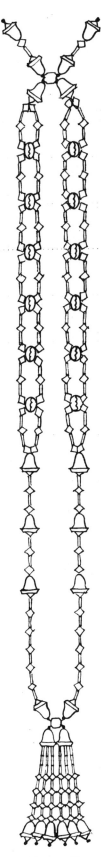

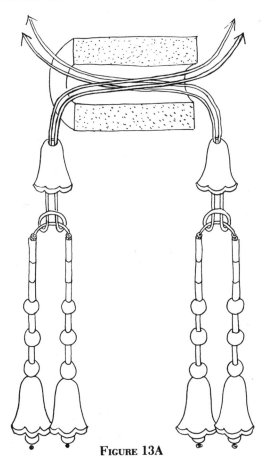

FIGURE 13A

FIGURE 13

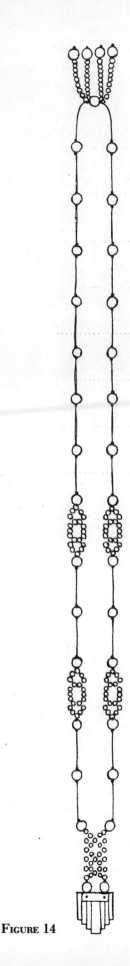

TWO-CORD NECKLACE: Bijou

FIGURE 14. 1 clear glass Deco bead at center front
33 clear glass round beads, 6 mm. in size
143 citron yellow round glass beads, 3 mm. in size

Strung and knotted on black silk thread (available at DRS; see Sources for Supplies).

SPECIAL INSTRUCTIONS

Run a long single thread through each of the two holes on the pendant—a long thread for the right side, and a long thread for the left. Center the pendant on each thread. Take the two free ends of the thread on the right side of the pendant and knot them immediately above the pendant. Take the two free ends of the thread on the left side of the pendant and knot them immediately above the pendant. Now you have two working threads for the right side of the necklace and two for the left. String the supporting band above the pendant bead, following the detailed diagram (Fig. 14A). *Note:* The three center beads in the interlacement producing this supporting band are in such a position that the hole, or bore, of each is horizontal.

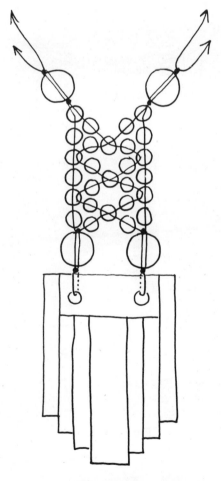

FIGURE 14   FIGURE 14A

The four decorative interlacement bands in the necklace (two on the right and two on the left) are similar to the interlacement described above. But they are simplified, since only two threads are used in the design. The bead beginning the design is threaded from each side so that its hole, or bore, is horizontal. The next four beads above the first bead, two on each side of the design, are threaded so their holes are in the usual vertical position. The two beads making the first bar across the design are strung with their holes in a horizontal position. Three vertical beads follow on each side of the design. Another bar of two horizontal beads crosses the design, and the final five beads ending the design mirror the first five beads, i.e., the last bead in that part of the design is again strung with its hole in a horizontal position.

THREE-CORD NECKLACE: Summer

FIGURE 15.   1 chalcedony-colored shell bead
30 frosted colorless drop beads, for the clusters
2 chalcedony beads, 8 mm. in size, above the clusters
10 frosted colorless tube beads between the Chinese three-cord knotting, 4 on each side, and 2 in the ending of the necklace
4 chalcedony beads, 6 mm. in size, for the ending of the necklace

Strung and knotted on chalcedony-colored silk cord.

Begin the necklace at center front. Pass the three cords through the shell bead, or whatever center pendant you decide to use. String the frosted drop beads to the right and left of the main bead. String five on each of the three cords on the right and five on each cord on the left. Thread the three cords on the right through a single round 8-mm. bead, then through a frosted tube bead. Using the three cords as one, tie an overhand knot. Thread the three cords on the left through a single round 8-mm. bead and then through a frosted tube bead. Pull the three cords on the left side of the necklace tight before tying them in an overhand knot. This will keep the center arrangement in its correct shape and tension.

Pin this finished part of the necklace in place on a corkboard. Work the left side of the necklace, following Figure 15. Tie a Solomon knot, left over right, right over left. Allow ¼" between this first knot and the second Solomon knot. Allow ¾" between the second Solomon knot and the third. Then allow

FIGURE 14B

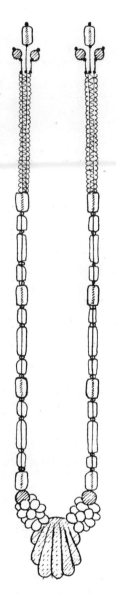

FIGURE 15

¼″ between the third Solomon knot and the fourth. String a bead, using all three cords as one. Before beginning the knotting again, make sure that the center cord of the three remains in the center, the right-hand cord on the right, and the left-hand cord on the left.

Repeat the spacing of Solomon knots given above. String another bead. Repeat the spacing of Solomon knots again. String another bead.

Finish the left side of the necklace with a band of Portuguese square or flat sinnit, i.e., one Solomon knot following another with no spaces between them, left over right, right over left, then left over right, right over left, etc. When the band is long enough for tying, end it by tying an overhand knot on each cord close against the last Solomon knot. Allow a space on each cord. Tie another overhand knot, string the appropriate bead on the cord, and finish each of the three cords with a figure-eight knot. Wet each knot with Duco cement and press the cement into the knot. Let the cement dry, then snip off the excess at the end of each of the three cords close to each knot. Seal each snipped end with an additional application of Duco cement.

Work the right side of the necklace in the same manner as the left, except that the Solomon knots should be tied right over left, left over right.

THREE-CORD NECKLACE: Prima Donna

FIGURE 16. 1 ox-blood-colored Peking glass bead, 24 mm. in size
5 ox-blood drop beads
8 ox-blood round beads, 6 mm. in size
24 clear beads, light gray tint, 6 mm. in size
14 clear cut-crystal beads, light gray tint, 6 x 10 mm. in size

Strung and knotted on black silk cord.

SPECIAL INSTRUCTIONS for stringing the three-cord necklace in FIGURE 16: Begin the necklace at the center front. Run three cords through the main bead. Center the bead on the cords.

Take one end—the working end of one cord—and string the pendant beads on it. Then run that same working end of that same cord through the main bead again, and tighten it with its pendant beads strung on it before knotting the three cords at each side of the main bead. String the other beads that make up the center front design. Then pin this finished part of the necklace in place on a corkboard. Work one side of the necklace, using right over left, then left over right for each Solomon knot, making two knots before and after each spaced bead. Allow ⅝″ between the knotted part of each space between beads.

Finish that side of the necklace with a band of Portuguese square or flat sinnit, i.e., Solomon knots, repeated, one after the other, until the band is as long as you want it to be for tying. Knot each cord independently at the end of the band of knots and finish each cord with a space, a knot, a bead, and a knot, as shown in Figure 16A.

Work the other side of the necklace, following the instructions given above, except that each Solomon knot is made with a *left over right, then right over left*, the opposite of the formula used in the completed side of the necklace.

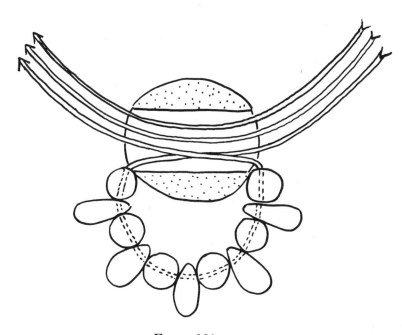

FIGURE 16A

FIGURE 16

FIGURE 17

THREE-CORD NECKLACE: Autumn

FIGURE 17. 1 cut-crystal smoky topaz bead, 24 mm. in size
30 frosted smoky topaz bell beads
30 clear smoky topaz beads, 6 mm. in size
20 clear smoky topaz beads, 8 mm. in size
7 frosted smoky topaz beads, 8 mm. in size

Strung and knotted on black silk cord.

Begin this necklace at the center back.

The ropelike parts in the drawing of this necklace are to indicate where the Portuguese spiral sinnit has been used. *Important:* On one side of the necklace a right-handed spiral sinnit—after being followed by a bead—is followed by another spiral sinit. This next sinnit *must* be a left-handed one in order to keep the necklace from twisting. In each spiral sinnit in the necklace the count must be even. It must also be the same, i.e., every sinnit must have four or six or eight left-handed half knots, or four or six or eight right-handed half knots, tied over the center cord.

The drawing of the parts of the necklace not tied in spiral sinnits represents flat sinnit tying—Solomon knots—with spaces between, i.e., two Solomon knots, space, two Solomon knots, space, two Solomon knots, space, two Solomon knots, and then the bead and spiral sinnit islands occur.

At center front, the three cords on the right go through the horizontal hole of the large "locking" bead and emerge on the left to be strung as a three-strand tassel. The three cords on the left go through the horizontal hole in the same locking bead and emerge on the right to be strung as a three-strand tassel.

Make sure before you string the necklace that the hole in the bead you want to use as the locking bead is large enough to let six cords pass through it.

Finish each tassel strand with a figure-eight knot. Apply Duco cement to the knots, and press it into each one. Snip off the excess cord. Cut close to the knot. Apply a small drop of Duco cement to each knot and let it dry.

Detailed instructions for three-cord knotting appear on pages 30 to 37.

BATIK BEADS

FIGURE 18.   3 drum-shaped Dutch trade beads, 15 x 18 mm.
        in size
    2 smaller Dutch trade beads, 12 x 15 mm. in size
    20 Dutch trade bead glass rings, 9 mm. in di-
        ameter
    2 Dutch trade bead glass rings, 16 mm. in di-
        ameter
    28 "stuffing" beads, tubular, 8 x 8 mm. in size

Strung IN *and* ON *old batik fabric spaghetti tubing.*

Cut fabric in two bias strips, 1½″ in width and about 18″ in length. Make a lengthwise center fold along each strip. Machine stitch ⅜″ away from this lengthwise fold. Turn the strips right side out. Use a bias spaghetti tube turner, available at most notion counters.

Cut a piece of thin strong string or cord about 25″ in length. Run it through one bias tube. Do not pull the string all the way through the tube. Allow both ends of the string to hang free. Apply Duco cement to the two ends of the string so as to stiffen them.

String a large-holed bead *on* the bias fabric tube. Then string a ring on either side of it. On the right side, take the stiffened end of the string that runs *through* the tube and string a stuffing bead on it. Slip the strung bead *into* the tube and guide it along the inside of the fabric tube until it hits the edge of the ring next to the large-holed bead. On the left side, take the stiffened end of the string that runs *through* the tube and string a stuffing bead on it. Slip the strung bead *into* the tube and guide it along the inside of the fabric tube until it hits the edge of the ring next to the large-holed bead.

String *on* and *inside* the hollow fabric tube following the pattern shown in Figure 18.

Attach this beaded front part of the necklace to two small rings. Sew the ends of the tube in place.

Sew the unbeaded bias tube to the two rings, adjusting the length of the necklace to suit your taste.

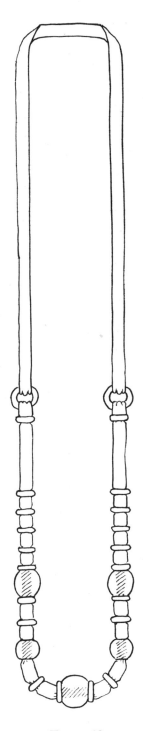

FIGURE 18

THE ULTIMATE NECKLACE

FIGURE 19.　1 glass heart
7 clear glass beads, 6 mm. in size
1 glass or obsidian ring

Strung and knotted on black silk cord using the Bosun's whistle knot, the Chinese butterfly knot, the single tatted chain, and simple whipping.

FIGURE 19

Earrings

Earrings can easily be made to match or go with any beaded necklace.

Use two 2-inch silver head-pins. Slip a bead on each pin. Make each earring as follows:

Take the round-nosed pliers and wind the top of the pin back on itself in a tight pigtail twist, as shown in Figure 20. Use the chain pliers to smooth the twist until it is round and neat. Use the clipping pliers to cut off the unused part of the silver pin. (See page 36.)

Slip each finished earring pendant on an S curve. (These should be of white or yellow gold. Your jeweler can make them to look like the one in the illustration.) Slide the pendant's loop along the S curve, from back to front (right to left on the diagram). It must cross the high arch on the S curve and drop to hang in the curve behind and below the ball, which keeps the pendant from falling off the S curve. Put the pointed end of the S curve through the pierced earlobe. Arrange it so that the upper curve of the S is hidden in the earlobe, and the pendant bead hangs below and slightly in front of the earlobe. To secure the earring, slip a friction ear nut on the part of the S curve left exposed behind the earlobe.

DRS (The Jewelers' Department Store, as it is called), is located at 15 West 47th Street, New York, New York 10036. They sell the pliers illustrated on page 38. They also carry silver head-pins, friction ear nuts, and many kinds of silver, gold-plated, and gold beads and findings, caps, and spring rings, etc.

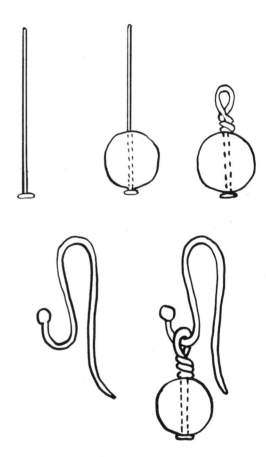

FIGURE 20

59

Japanese Bag–Tesage

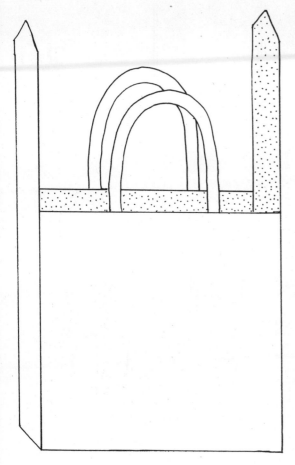

FIGURE 21

FIGURE 21

FOR THE OUTSIDE

    Cut one piece of fabric 24″ x 11½″, two pieces 19″ x 3″, pointing one end of each piece, as shown on the diagram. Cut two pieces 14″ x 2½″.

FOR THE LINING

    Cut one piece of fabric 24″ x 11½″, and two pieces 19″ x 3″, pointing one end of each piece, as shown in Figure 21.

    At each end of the large piece of fabric for the bag (and also at each end of the large piece of fabric for the lining) fold in the ½″ seam allowance, and press along the fold line. On each piece clip to the seam line at A, A, A, and A. Sew each side gusset to the large piece, from A to A. Sew side gussets to sides of bag, from A to B. Turn bag right side out. Sew the two lining side gussets to the lining from A to A, and then from A to B, following the directions given for sewing the bag.

    Keep lining inside out. Slip right-side-out bag into inside-out lining. Sew lining-side gussets to bag-side gussets from B to C to D to C to B. Pull bag out of lining. Push inside-out lining into right-side-out bag. Find and pull out the two pointed side gussets that you have sewn together—i.e., bag gusset to lining gusset at each end of the bag—and turn them right side out.

    Fold handle pieces along the fold line, from E to E. Sew each handle from F to F. Clip off excess fabric. Turn handles right side out. Pin handles to folded top of lining from E to F. Baste in place. Pin folded top of bag to folded top of lining, from B to B, catching in the handle ends. Topstitch the bag to the lining from B to B on each side, sewing ⅛″ from the edge. Stitch a second row of topstitching ⅛″ away from the first row of topstitching. Lay the bag flat as shown in the diagram and tie the pointed side gussets together in a square knot.

To make beaded handles, follow the directions given for batik beads (page 57). Make the handles 14″ long. The beaded part should be no more than 13″ in length. This will give you a ½″-inch seam allowance at each end of the handle. Sew the bag as described above.

Pockets may be sewn to the sides of the lining. And if you want to stiffen the bottom of the bag, cut a piece of sturdy cardboard 2″ x 10½″, and cover it with the lining fabric. Slip it into the bottom of the finished bag.

NOTE: All gusset-seam allowances should be pressed toward the gusset, away from the bag.

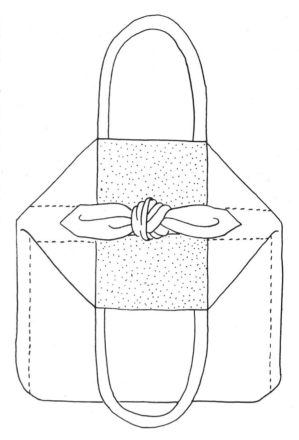

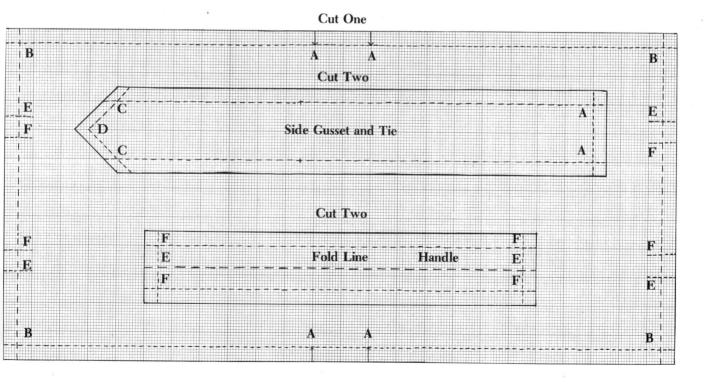

FIGURE 22

Sources for Supplies

FOR CORD AND THREAD

Margot Gallery
26 West 54th Street
New York, N.Y. 10019

FOR BEADS

Bead-L-Caravan
16 West 55th Street
New York, N.Y. 10019

Ellis Import Co., Inc.
44 West 37th Street
New York, N.Y. 10018

DiMar Import Co.
4 West 37th Street
New York, N.Y. 10018

York Novelty Import, Inc.
10 West 37th Street
New York, N.Y. 10018

DRS
15 West 47th Street
New York, N.Y. 10036

FOR ANTIQUE LARGE-HOLED BEADS
(while they last)

Craft Caravan, Inc.
127 Spring Street
New York, N.Y. 10012

Trudy Seligman
82 West 12th Street
New York, N.Y. 10011

Bibliography

ASHLEY, CLIFFORD W. *The Ashley Book of Knots.* Garden City, N.Y.: Doubleday, Doran & Co., 1944.

GLASSMAN, JUDITH. *Beadcraft, Step by Step.* New York: Golden Press, 1974.

GRAUMONT, RAOUL, AND HENSEL, JOHN. *Encyclopedia of Knots and Fancy Rope Work.* New York: Cornell Maritime Press, 1952.

SHAW, GEORGE RUSSELL. *Knots, Useful and Ornamental.* New York: Macmillan, 1972.

WALLER, IRENE. *Knots and Netting.* New York: Taplinger Publishing Co., 1977.